Columbus

Shashi Ambaru

Prodigy

Columbus

First Edition: December 2009
80 Pages
Printed in India.

ISBN 978-81-8493-322-2

Pro-ya-en-58

Prodigy Books is an imprint of
New Horizon Media Pvt. Ltd.
177/103, First Floor,
Ambal's Building, Lloyds Road,
Royapettah, Chennai 600 014.
Ph: +91-44-4200-9603

Email : support@nhm.in
Website : www.nhm.in

Prodigy is an imprint of New Horizon Media Private Limited

Content

The Journey towards Knowledge

Among the many qualities and characteristics that are inherent in man, curiosity is the most natural and universal of all. Curiosity is often regarded with a negative eye. Inquisitiveness and a desire to poke into others' matters are the undesirable effects of curiosity. But one should not overlook the great potential and capacity that leads man from curiosity to knowledge.

The notable scientist and Nobel winner, Aaron Klug said, *'Human curiosity, the urge to know, is a powerful force and is perhaps the best secret weapon of all in the struggle to unravel the workings of the natural world.'* Nowhere does curiosity play a major role than in the field of science, technology and discovery. Some of the most important inventions and discoveries in the history of mankind would not have been possible without the element of curiosity.

A curious mind is often the hallmark of a great intellect. Without a questioning nature, would Newton have wondered about the falling apple and discovered gravity? Was it not curiosity and a passion to know that propelled geniuses like Einstein and Edison towards discovering and making major breakthroughs in science?

Often, it is deemed that children are the most curious of all beings. A child with its wide-eyed innocence regards the whole world as a place of learning. He seeks to learn, know and find about anything that spurs his curiosity. This inimitable quality is retained even in adulthood only by few. These are the few men and women who look beyond the obvious and strive towards knowing what is unknown. The annals of history abound with stories of great scientists, discoverers and explorers who dared to think about and perform the seemingly impossible.

It is due to these great thinkers that immense progress has been made and is being made in the fields of science and technology. It is a curious mind which looks at a lantern and wonders if light cannot be produced electrically. Only a curious mind will question the theory that said that the

Sun revolved around the Earth and not vice versa. It is the mind that seeks knowledge that toils towards finding a cure for the diseases it sees in the world. Only a mind that has courage and curiosity looks at the sea and wonders what lies beyond the horizon.

Right from the primitive ages, man has always striven towards learning new things. This has been seen in the invention of the wheel and the discovery of fire. Just as scientific discoveries have been made since several centuries, there is another field of discovery that goes back to 380 B.C. This is the field of *exploration*. Exploration is the pursuit or search for unknown lands and people for the purpose of knowledge or material gain.

Explorers of yore travelled the seas in search of new land for the sole purpose of commercial gain. Curiosity led these men to brave the turbulent seas and discover unchartered territories and new cultures. As discovery of new lands led to the knowledge of the goods found there, the concept of trade routes by sea was established. Great emperors also sought to reinforce their military might by conquering and ruling the newfound lands.

The period between the fifteenth and the nineteenth centuries is termed as the *Age of Exploration* or *Age of Discovery*. The time saw several Europeans travel across the oceans in search of viable trade partners and goods. Due to their endeavour, there were many developments in navigation techniques and shipbuilding. In their pursuit of valuable goods such as gold, silver and spices, these ancient explorers also became responsible for the discovery of several present day countries and continents. Perhaps the most significant of these discoveries was the finding of the American continents by an intrepid explorer and navigator named Christopher Columbus.

Early Days

The history of the great discoverer of the American continents began in a small town in the country of Italy. Columbus is widely regarded to have been born in a place called Genoa (also known as Genova). It can be no surprise that the seafarer had his roots in this town which is situated on the coastline of the Italian peninsula.

If one searches for this place on a map, one will see the interesting location of Genoa on the coastline. The coast is in the shape of a bent human knee and Genoa is located exactly at the point where it bends at an angle. Thus, the name originated from the word 'knee' in the ancient language of the Ligurians, who inhabited the place.

The geographical position of Genoa afforded it an important place in the early Christian era. Located as it was along the shore, its maritime possibilities were abundant. Thus, it was an ideal town for trading and business through the seas. Apart from its commercial viability, it was natural that it was also home to several adventurers and seafaring men. But Columbus' ancestors did not have any legacy of sailing. Instead they were weavers by profession.

During the early fourteenth and fifteenth centuries, there was frequent migration along the shores of the Mediterranean. Columbus' grandfather, Giovanni Colombo had settled down in a village east of Genoa in the year 1429. His son, Domenico was sent to Genoa to serve as an apprentice under a weaver there. After completing his apprenticeship and he had settled in Genoa.

In 1440, Domenico married Sussannah Fontanarossa, the daughter of another weaver. It was the mid-fifteenth century when Columbus was born to them in Genoa. The exact date of his birth has been a matter of dispute among historians. But the popular version contends his birth to have taken place between August 25 and the end of October in the year 1451.

Columbus may not have been the first child to his parents. But it is believed that if there were any older siblings, they did not survive. He however had four younger siblings. Bartholomew was born a couple of years after him. Giovanni was his second brother who died young. Columbus had one sister, Bianchinetta. However, there is nothing known about her. His youngest brother, Giacomo (also known as Diego) is supposed to be almost seventeen years younger to him.

Columbus' father, Domenico was a noteworthy personality who occupied a moderately good position in the lower middle class society in Genoa. He was perceived as an enthusiastic man who undertook several ventures, which were often unsuccessful. His vigour and enterprise may have passed on to Columbus. But historians believe that Domenico lacked the determination and willpower that his son had.

Columbus and his brother, Bartholomew helped their father in the business of weaving. The early years of Columbus as a child and teen are shrouded in mystery. Not much is known about his education and life for the first fifteen years. Around eighteen years of age, he was seen as a tall young man with a crop of red hair.

In the year 1470, Domenico was sent to a neighbouring seaport, Savona, by the gild of clothiers. He was assigned to learn the rules and methods of the weavers there. After his visit to Savona, Domenico realized that operating his business in Savona would profit him more than in Genoa. So he decided to move his trade and family to the new place. In Savona, Domenico also acted as a wine merchant, along with his regular trade as a weaver.

Though it is believed that Columbus had no formal education in his childhood, he evinced interest in maritime adventures from an early age. Some evidence points to his travel on an expedition at the age of ten. Columbus himself claims, in his writings, to have been on his first voyage in 1461. In 1472, it is also believed that he served as one of the seamen on a ship under the service of René of Anjou, which was sent to capture a galley (an ancient ship operated entirely by men for the purpose of warfare and trade), named *Fernandina*.

The Beginning

The passion for the sea in Columbus can be attributed to the early years of his residence in Genoa and then in Savona. Genoa was a hub of maritime activity. The coastline was dotted with innumerable harbours and coves, where ships were built and many galleys laid anchor or set sail. Another significant reason for its popularity was the presence of several mapmakers.

During the early centuries, when navigation techniques were still not sophisticated, sailors sought the help of charts prepared by these mapmakers. These charts were called *portolan charts*. These were maps describing the physical features of the ports and harbours along the Mediterranean.

They helped the mariners to distinguish and recognize a particular port. The portolan charts were made in Italy and Spain. The pioneers and leaders of exploration at that time were the Portuguese. Hence, Genoa often saw the Portuguese on its shores seeking the services of the mapmakers for their voyages.

Such a vibrant marine atmosphere would surely have affected even the least imaginative youngster in Genoa. The stories of sailors and their adventures must have inspired countless dreams in the eyes of young boys. Thus, it was not a matter of wonder that Columbus was stung by the sailing bug. Even though not properly schooled, he must have picked up nuggets of practical knowledge from his surroundings. But, in spite of his leaning towards sailing, it cannot be denied that his childhood and most of his teenage was spent as a dutiful son serving in the family business.

While Columbus' life took its own course after a few years in Savona, Domenico returned to Genoa around 1483 with Bianchinetta and Giacomo. His wife, Sussannah and son, Giovanni, had passed away during their stay in Savona. Bianchinetta was married off to a cheesemonger. Columbus and his brother, Bartholomew meanwhile had embarked on their own ways of life. Bartholomew had become a mapmaker and he resided in the city of Lisbon in Portugal. Giacomo would follow the footsteps of his brother, Columbus, and join him on his future voyages. It is not known when Domenico passed away but the last record of his existence was in 1494.

Before his father left Savona, Columbus had joined as an apprentice in a merchant banking company, owned by the Centurione, di Negro and Spinola families of Genoa. The company sent several expeditions with the purpose of financial development of its concerns. At that time, the Greek island, Chios was famous for mastic gum, used as a spice and for flavouring. The Genoese had complete control over the trade of mastic gum. Hence, the Centurione sent its ships to Chios for trade. Columbus could have travelled to Chios on any of the two voyages which took place in 1474 and '75.

Even though Columbus might have had his first taste of adventure in the ship of René, it can be certain that his hands-on experience on the voyage to Chios would have taught him much more about navigation. Most of his early knowledge would have come from these practical lessons than from any scholarly learning.

During that time, the Mediterranean was in a state of unrest. Most of the countries were at war in a bid for dominance and power. Around this time, in 1476, Columbus was on board another ship that was a part of a fleet. These vessels were intended to carry the supplies of mastic gum for trade in Lisbon and England. The ships were sailing just off the coast of Portugal when they were suddenly attacked by an enemy fleet. A fierce sea battle ensued. Some ships collapsed while hundreds of men drowned. Columbus himself was injured but he managed to reach the shore of Lagos, from where he finally reached Lisbon.

This misadventure, if it may be called so, would eventually turn out to be a starting point for Columbus' future voyages. Reaching Lisbon was a blessing for him. Lisbon, the capital of Portugal, was a very important city during those times. The Portugese, being the pioneers of maritime exploration, obviously made their capital city a hub for their activities. Thus, Lisbon was at the center of the storm of adventure and exploration taking place at that time. Moreover, for Columbus, the presence of his brother, Bartholomew was an added advantage for him.

Around 1477, Columbus is regarded to have undertaken a voyage towards the north. His writings have led historians to believe that he might have travelled to Ireland and from there to Iceland. This might have spurred him on to further exploration but it is a claim that has no evidence. After his return to Lisbon, Columbus joined hands with his brother in the latter's mapmaking business. Apart from that, he also got opportunities to learn everything that he would need to know as a seafarer.

It was here that he learnt the languages of the seamen, which were Portugese and Castilian. He also began to learn Latin which was the language of the ancient geographical texts. For navigation purposes, he gained knowledge in mathematics and astronomy. As his brother's partner, he soon established himself as a creditable mapmaker. Thus, his stay in Portugal equipped him for his future endeavours.

Columbus is said to have resided in Portugal for a period of eight or nine years. Within a few years in Lisbon, Columbus managed to form a good reputation among the people there. An example of this was his subsequent marriage to Dona Felipa Perestrello Moniz. Her father, Bartholomew Perestrello and mother, Dona Isabel Moniz belonged to noble families.

Planning and Preparation

After their marriage, Columbus and his wife stayed for some time in Porto Santo, an island in Portugal. It was here that their son, Diego was born. It is also believed that they resided at a neighbouring island, Madeira. The house that they lived in Porto Santo now stands as a museum exhibiting his artifacts. Not much is known about what happened to Columbus' wife after this period.

In 1481, the King's death led to the coronation of John II as the King of Portugal. The young King was responsible for reviving the economy of the country. But more importantly, with respect to exploration, his reign was a blessing. After coming to power, John II encouraged exploration of

Africa and the East. With his benevolent attitude towards maritime exploration, explorers were given a generous hearing.

Meanwhile, Columbus might have travelled on an expedition to Guinea. This time, he could have attained sufficient reputation to have been in an important position of an officer or a master. His experiences on these voyages taught him many aspects of maritime navigation. Soon, his travels had instilled in him the desire to discover the unknown and the unexplored.

A key element in most explorations at that time was the establishment of trade routes to Asia, or the Indies as it was called then. Previous to John II, there was his great-uncle, Prince Henry of Portugal who expressed a keen interest in navigation and exploration. Under his patronage, several mapmakers and navigators flourished in Portugal. It was on his behest that the Portugese empire, then headed by his father, John I, conquered Ceuta, the commercial center of North Africa.

After establishing control over the lucrative trade in Africa, Prince Henry aimed at finding a way to circumnavigate the southern tip of Africa. This would serve his purpose of charting a direct trade route by sea towards the Far East. He initiated several expeditions to Africa during his time. He was also responsible for the creation of a new kind of ship, named the *caravel*. The caravel was lighter and better suited to the long voyages that were envisioned by explorers. Prince Henry's contributions to these navigational innovations and exploration earned him the name of *Henry the Navigator*. Sadly, during his lifetime, his dream of finding a way around the tip of Africa was not achieved.

Another important event that necessitated the discovery of a sea route to Asia was the fall of Constantinople in 1453. Constantinople was a crucial link for trade by land between Europe and Asia. The city was seized by Muslim Turks with whom the Christian empires in Europe did not enjoy a good relation. Thus, the vital land route to Asia was closed for the Europeans who then had to seek an alternative sea route to the Far East.

The considerable travels that Columbus had undertaken before 1480 had given him a sense of what he could achieve. He began to envision a plan to travel to the East, which he called '*Enterprise of the Indies*'.

However, the point where he differed from most of the other explorers was his plan to travel west in order to reach the east. The idea was not original but it had never been executed before. To understand his intention, it is important to know the geographical theories that were extant at that time.

It was an accepted fact that the earth was spherical in shape. The Greeks and Romans believed that there was a single body of water that connected Europe and Asia. It was also thought that there was no existing land between the two continents. Hence, by travelling west, one could reach the east. However, no one had a clear idea of the distance that had to be covered.

Ptolemy, an ancient astronomer, geographer and mathematician, had provided instructions on constructing maps of the existing, known lands in the world. For a long time, his writings, originally in Greek, did not attain much importance. But, in the early fifteenth century, they were published in Latin which resulted in their widespread popularity.

Ptolemy postulated that the earth as a sphere was covered by 180 degrees of land and the rest by water. He also believed that further discovery could be made by exploring the west rather than the north or the south. While Columbus agreed with most of Ptolemy's assertions, he believed that the known land covered more than 180 degrees of earth. He was influenced more by Ptolemy's predecessor, Marinus of Tyre, who wrongly assessed that the landmass covered around 225 degrees of earth. Therefore, Columbus believed that he would have to travel a shorter distance across the sea to reach the east.

Columbus' beliefs were reinforced by coming to know about the similar ideas espoused by Toscanelli, an Italian mathematician, astronomer and cosmographer. Toscanelli had chalked out a map which outlined his conviction that Asia could be reached by sailing west. He had sent this map through one of his acquaintances to the King of Portugal in 1474. Somehow, Columbus heard of his ideas and corresponded with Toscanelli, requesting him for the outline of his scheme. According to Toscanelli, it would take only 3000 nautical miles to reach the east.

Columbus erred in his calculations of the circumference of the earth and also the narrowness of the ocean separating Europe and Asia. He based his calculations on the writings of a Persian astronomer, Alfraganus. Alfraganus used Arabic miles to estimate the circumference while Columbus mistook them for Italian miles. The Arabic miles were longer than the Italian miles. Thus, Columbus from his wrong calculations, designated the circumference of the earth at around 25,255 kilometers. However, the actual circumference is around 40,000 kilometers.

Apart from his experiences on sea, Columbus was also inspired by several books which he had read over the course of years. Among the books which influenced him were - *Imago Mundi* written by Cardinal d'Ailly, which was an extensive book on geographical knowledge; the *Travels of Marco Polo*, detailing the journey of Marco Polo through Asia; and Pliny's *Naturalis Historia*, an encyclopedia.

For many years, the idea of travelling and exploring the west was brewing in the mind of Columbus. He also received a wealth of information due to his marriage. His father-in-law, Bartholomew Perestrello was himself a navigator and explorer. Under Prince Henry's initiation, he along with other Portuguese sailors had discovered the Madeira islands. After Perestrello's demise, all his maps, papers, charts and journals came to the hands of Columbus. These papers gave Columbus detailed knowledge of the winds and currents along the Atlantic.

By the early 1480s, Columbus had slowly and surely formulated his plan to travel in the west. It was now time to seek outside support for his idea. Exploration could not be done without financial endorsement from the royalty. During those times, it was essential that the reigning monarch approved and supported the voyagers. Exploration did not end with the discovery of a place. It was necessary to establish relations with the people and gain control over the land and its goods. For this, it was important to have the encouragement of a ruler, who had adequate military and political power.

Hence, Columbus decided to put forward his plans to the monarchs of his time. The presence of John II at the helm of Portugal was conducive to Columbus' intentions. It was only natural that he would first apply himself to the patronage of the King of Portugal. He had by then earned quite a good reputation, thanks to his work for the merchant banking concern. Moreover, his marriage into the noble family of Perestrello enabled him to establish contact with the court and the King.

As John II was known for his encouragement to explorers, Columbus decided to take his scheme to the King's presence. Though Columbus had been chalking out his plan for a long time, he could not approach the King who was then dealing with conspiracy and rebellion within the kingdom. However, by 1484, the King had completely established his power and Columbus immediately took his plans to him. But it would not be an easy matter for Columbus' plans to come to fruition so soon.

The Struggle for Support

In the year 1484, Columbus sought an audience with John II to outline his scheme to reach the Indies by travelling through the west. He sketched out his ideas giving the King his research, calculations and reasons for formulating the plan of action. His aim was to sail in the west in order to reach the Indies, which included India and the island nation, Cipango (Japan).

Another matter of dispute among historians is the claim that Columbus had demanded certain privileges from the King with regard to his voyage. How far this was true cannot be determined but Columbus had managed to make an impression on the King. The King then agreed to look into his plans and as a result, he referred the matter to the Maritime Advisory Committee.

The council comprised three people - two Jewish physicians, Roderigo and José Vizinho, and a bishop, Diogo Ortiz de Vilhegas. The committee quickly disproved Columbus' assertions. They contended that he had underestimated the distance to be covered and in general, he was a fanciful adventurer who based his extravagant scheme on inaccuracies.

Whether the King rejected Columbus' plan based on the advice of his committee or due to Columbus' demands is not known, but Columbus returned empty-handed from the King's court. However, the King did not utterly discourage him. He assured Columbus to return to him at a later time in case other voyages which he had previously commissioned were unsuccessful. But Columbus was disappointed and decided to try his luck in Spain.

The following year, Columbus left Portugal for Spain with his son, Diego. His wife's demise was thought to have occurred by then. Columbus left Portugal in a secretive manner owing to his incurring several debts in the country.

When Columbus arrived in Spain by mid-1485, the country was in a state of turmoil. Spain was then ruled by Ferdinand

II of Aragon and his wife, Isabella of Castile. Their marriage had united the several kingdoms that were till then ruled separately. The King and Queen were engaged in a long-drawn war with the Muslim-ruled Kingdom of Granada. They were stationed at Cordova, the headquarters from where the monarchs were directing the war.

When he first reached Spain, Columbus went to a monastery, named La Rabida. The monks who resided there had an active interest in navigation. Here Columbus became acquainted with Fray Antonio de Marchena, who proved to be a great support to his endeavours.

In January 1486, Columbus arrived at Cordova to apply to the monarchs, who were also known as the Catholic Sovereigns. But he was late as they had left for Madrid by then. He had no other alternative than to wait for their return. During this time, Columbus met Beatriz Enriquez de Harana, with whom he had a son, named Ferdinand.

Around May, the monarchs returned to Cordova and Columbus got an opportunity to present his case before them. Columbus' assertions and grand schemes did not impress the Sovereigns who were already under the great stress of the war. Here, Columbus received the help of his friend, Antonio de Marchena, who pleaded the monarchs to at least set up a committee to look into the plan in detail.

Accordingly, the Queen ordered an inquiry to be made into the feasibility of Columbus' ideas. The chief member of this committee was Talavera, who was assigned the task of securing the opinions of the noted cosmographers in Castile. While the inquiry took its own time, the court allowed Columbus a pension of 12,000 maravedis a year. (A maravedi is a coin of gold or silver, which was the currency at that time.)

During this waiting period, Columbus made another important friend, Diego de Deza. The committee headed by Talavera adjourned its meetings from Cordova to Salamanca around Christmas. Salamanca was a university town, consisting of many residential colleges. The committee held its meetings during the winter in one of these colleges, St. Stephen. Diego de Deza was the prior of the college at that time. Deza became an ardent supporter of Columbus.

In August 1487, the Sovereigns captured an important seaport, Malaga. Columbus saw an opportunity in this momentary victory and proceeded there to plead his case with the monarchs again. Unfortunately, the thought of war was paramount on their minds and hence, they did not encourage Columbus in any way. Columbus returned disheartened. The wait became more prolonged and frustrating for him the next year as the court lost complete interest in his project. Around mid-1488, the small pension that he was receiving was also stopped, leading to further disillusionment.

Meanwhile, Bartholomew intimated to Columbus that the situation at Portugal appeared to be favourable. A Portugese explorer, Bartholomeu Diaz had been sent by John II in 1487 to find a route to India by circumnavigating the tip of Africa. However, there was no word from him by early 1488. So, Columbus applied to the Portugal King for a chance to hear him out again. John II cordially replied to his request and asked him to come to Lisbon without the fear of being pursued by his creditors.

Columbus did not immediately leave for Portugal in the anticipation of a positive response from his long-pending application with the committee at Spain. But as days went by, he realized that the wait was proving to be futile. By December 1488, Columbus reached Lisbon. Unfortunately for him, while he was there, the fleet headed by Bartholomeu Diaz returned successful from its voyage.

Diaz was victorious in travelling around the tip of Africa. He discovered the Cape of Good Hope, considered to be the southern point where travel begins towards the east than the south.

The ambition of John II to circumnavigate the southern tip of Africa was accomplished with the success of Diaz's venture. This gave the Portugese a possibility to explore the sea route to the east by travelling towards the south. Hence, they did not require to find any other route by travelling west.

Columbus' hopes were thwarted and he had to return to Spain disappointed. He was back in Spain by 1489. Before he left the place, it is believed that he urged his brother, Bartholomew to seek the support of the King of England, Henry VII. However, no positive response was obtained from the English King as well.

After his return from Portugal, it is not known how but Columbus managed to get an interview with the Queen who was then alone at Jaén. The King was engaged in battle at Baza. The discussions with the Queen left Columbus with the impression that he might gain their support once Granada was conquered. Columbus, who was nearly broke then, was given a letter endorsed by the Sovereigns. This letter instructed all officials to furnish him with food and lodging for his transportation. In December, 1489, Baza was under the control of the Sovereigns. Once again, the Queen's attention was diverted from Columbus' plan to the war.

Meanwhile, Columbus frequented the monastery, La Rabida and maintained his friendship with Fray Antonio, who directed him to Dukes of Medina Sidonia and Medina Celi. These were noblemen who headed independent territories along the sea coast of Spain. They were entitled to several privileges but were answerable to the King. Both these Dukes had several ships under their control and hence, it was felt that their acquaintance would help further Columbus' cause.

Columbus first tried his luck with the Duke of Medina Sidonia, who had many prosperous ventures. However, most of his ships were already engaged in the war with Granada. The Duke was not impressed with the grand schemes of Columbus and did not express any interest in supporting his claims. The Duke of Medina Celi, on the other hand, seemed more conducive to his ideas and venture.

In fact, he was so impressed that he offered Columbus not only money and food but also lodging at his house. Columbus would enjoy his patronage for two more years.

The Duke had complete faith in Columbus' vision. At one point of time, he even considered sending his own ships as a part of Columbus' expedition. However, without the approval of the Sovereigns, he could not undertake such a monumental enterprise alone. Meanwhile, around the year 1490, Columbus' brother, Bartholomew, had taken his plans to the King of France, Charles VIII.

Though he could not find favour with the King, Bartholomew found a kindly ear in the King's sister, Anne de Beaujeu. Hence, his hopes were not completely dashed.

Meanwhile, the Duke of Medina Celi personally wrote to the Queen outlining his interest in Columbus' scheme and his support to the navigator's claims. The Queen graciously replied to his letter, citing her pleasure at his full-fledged support for Columbus. But she believed that such an enterprise as envisioned by Columbus could only be fulfilled by monarchs, and not noblemen. Hence, the Duke's request was summarily rejected. However, the Sovereigns pressed the committee to give their final decision.

The opinions of this committee did not differ much from that of the committee in Portugal. The members of the Castile council also came to the conclusion that Columbus was mistaken in believing the distance of the ocean between Spain and the Indies to be short. However, possibly due to Deza's belief in Columbus, the Sovereigns did not summarily dismiss him. Instead, they assured him that their decision could be altered at a later time when they would be freed from the struggles of war.

This final blow to his plans after a long and fruitless wait dejected Columbus. He decided to approach the King of France, whose favour was being continuously sought by his brother. In 1491, on his way to France with his son, Diego, he stopped at la Rabida for food. At that time, the prior was Fray Juan Pérez, who had been confessor of the Queen. When he came to know about Columbus' plans and intention to approach the King of France, he offered to help Columbus in convincing the Sovereigns.

The prior extended the hospitality of the convent to Columbus and his son. He then sent a messenger to the Queen, who was then at Santa Fé, to listen to Columbus for one last time. The Queen sent for the prior to have a personal consultation. The prior was vehement in his support to Columbus' ideas. Convinced by him, the Queen commanded Columbus to meet her. She also sent money with the messenger for his clothing and travel.

When Columbus arrived, the long-drawn war had finally come to a close and the Spanish monarchs had conquered the Kingdom of Granada. The whole place was jubilant and brimming with celebrations. With the war behind them, the monarchs were ready to give a patient hearing to Columbus. When he saw that they were favourably disposed to his scheme, Columbus put forward before them the following conditions:

1. That he would be granted three caravels loaded and equipped with goods sufficient for one year;

2. That he would be given the title of 'Great Admiral of the Ocean';

3. That he should be appointed Governor of any islands or lands that he might discover;

4. That he would have the right to one-tenth of the revenue that might be earned from any of the goods that would be found on the discovered lands.

These demands were deemed to be preposterous and the monarchs refused to agree to them. Dejected and frustrated, Columbus left Santa Fé on a mule.

The royal treasurer, Santangel, who had become his friend, sought the Queen and eloquently urged her to reconsider their decision. He argued that if the venture was a failure, they would not be at a loss. Yet, if it were taken up by a rival nation and became a success, Spain's loss would be immense. His remonstrances worked and the Queen decided to support the Enterprise. Immediately, a messenger was sent to intercept Columbus on his journey.

Columbus was at Pinos-Puente when he received the good news from the messenger. Though the plan was approved, it took almost three months for it to be put in action. On April 17, 1492, the conditions were laid out and duly signed. Thus, after a long and often frustrating struggle, Columbus finally was set to go on his first voyage.

Departure of the first voyage from the port of Palos, by Evaristo Dominguez

The First Voyage

On 12 May 1492, Columbus reached the town of Palos, from where he would begin his first voyage. The Sovereigns ordered the community of Palos to help Columbus by supplying two caravels and sufficient crew members to accompany the expedition, within a period of ten days. This was not such an easy task as Columbus discovered soon. The people of Palos were hostile to the venture as they had to fund the expenditure of the two caravels on their own. But, as subjects to the monarchs' authority, they had no other alternative.

The town supplied two caravels, named *Niña* and *Pinta*. But Columbus had to furnish another ship, *Santa Maria* at his own expense. He could do this with the help of the Pinzón brothers, who were navigators and shipowners. The people were unwilling to enlist as crew for what they thought was a doomed voyage. Here, Fray Juan Perez helped by encouraging the men to join as the crew for the expedition. All these delays ensured that the ships were completely ready only after ten weeks.

Columbus was at the head of the major ship, *Santa Maria.* The two caravels were under the leadership of the Pinzón brothers - *Pinta* under Martin Alonzo Pinzón and *Niña* under Viñcente Yaòez Pinzón. Just before daybreak on August 3 , 1492, the three ships set sail. The fleet began to travel in a southwesterly direction with its first stop being the Canary Islands, a Spanish archipelago.

On the way, *Pinta* faced problems with its structure but under the able command of Martin Alonzo, the ship was able to reach the port of Canary Islands by August 12. However, the ship was in dire need of repairs and seemed to be incapable of continuing the voyage. Columbus tried to secure another ship in its place but failed. Hence, he was forced to stay at the port until *Pinta* was repaired and was deemed worthy to travel in the long expedition. This unexpected event delayed the fleet's voyage till September 6. On that day, the fleet continued its journey from the port of Gomera.

From here on, the voyage began. Most of the crew did not have complete confidence in Columbus' vision. They were doubtful and apprehensive that the fleet would discover any new lands. Whenever Columbus felt that the crew would be weary of the long travel, he would misrepresent the actual figures of the distance they had travelled that day. Sometimes, however, the crew would find signs that led them to believe that they would sight land.

During the tiring days of endless seafaring, the crew would spot tropical birds which would never travel very far from land. They would also notice patches of weed that gave them the impression of having been washed from land into the sea. These indications forced the initially reluctant crew members to believe in the mission of the voyage. As days went on, these occasional appearances of birds and seaweed strengthened their belief of finding land.

On September 25, Martin Alonzo called out aloud from *Pinta* that he could see land afar. It led to general excitement and great joy as the crew members climbed on to the sails to confirm his statement. Columbus was overcome with relief and commanded the fleet to follow the course towards the land. But by the next day, the men realized that it had been a false alarm. What they had thought was land was actually a mass of clouds.

This disappointing event further disillusioned the crew and increased their animosity towards Columbus. Days went on with each day being no different than the other. Three weeks had gone by on the sea with no hint of land anywhere. It was with great difficulty that the captains of the three ships maintained calm and control over the sullen crew members. Soon, it was October. Martin Alonzo then urged Columbus to change the direction of the fleet from west to a southwesterly direction.

On October 7, there came a second false alarm when crew members once again thought that they had sighted land. Columbus was by then flustered with the illusions of land. Waiting till sunset, when no land came in sight, he decided to alter the fleet's course from SW to WSW. He took this decision basing on the flight of the tropical birds which they continued to see. He thought that it was advisable to follow the course of the birds in order to find land.

The next few days, the fleet followed the birds in the southwestward direction. This change in the course of the fleet did not bring any cheer to the crew. In spite of Columbus' assurances, they knew that according to his calculations, they should have reached land long before. The crew also were fearful of being unable ever to return home. On October 10, fearing a mutiny from the crew, Columbus promised them that he would direct the fleet back home if they did not sight land within two or three days.

The crew was momentarily quelled by this assurance. The next day however brought a great change in their attitude and an immense relief to Columbus. This was due to the appearance of several indications of approaching land. Several objects were found floating in the sea which gave every sign of a land nearby. On the night of October 11, Columbus exclaimed that he could see a glimmer of light far away. But he was not sure that it was indeed a sign of land. Other crew members were doubtful and were not certain that they could see any light.

A few hours later, at 2 a.m., the seaman who was on the lookout on *Pinta,* Rodrigo de Triana, shouted that he could see land. Alerted by his cry, Martin Alonzo verified the truth of his statement. Joyous to notice land which was not imaginary for the first time, he fired a signal that communicated the news to the other ships. Columbus was delighted and ordered the fleet to sail towards the land, which was around six miles away.

The land that Columbus and his fleet landed upon was the eastern coast of what is now the Bahamas. For the first time, a European had stepped on a land in the Western Hemisphere. The land was named by Columbus as *San*

Columbus claims the New World by the Prang Education Company

Salvador. Though there have been other contenders in the Bahamas which claim to have been the land first discovered by Columbus, the island that fits the description accurately is present-day San Salvador or Watling's Island.

Columbus and the captains of the other two ships first set foot on the island, carrying the banners of the expedition. The boat on which they arrived also displayed the royal standard of the Catholic Sovereigns. Some of the crew members followed the captains. They noticed several native Indians, who seemed to be of a friendly disposition. The natives called the island 'Guanahani'. Then in the presence of the captains, crew and the few Indians gathered there, Columbus took possession of the island, renamed San Salvador, for the King and the Queen.

The crew members were jubilant at having finally discovered a new land. They accepted Columbus as their Admiral and all their ill-will towards him vanished. To the crew's surprise, the natives were very mild, guileless and friendly towards them. Columbus gave several small trinkets to the natives who in return brought the crew something in exchange. The natives appeared to be primitive in their lifestyle.

Columbus highlighted these virtues later in his Letter to the Sovereigns. These qualities of the natives were partly suitable to the purpose of the expedition. One of the reasons, if not the most important, that the monarchs supported such voyages was the possibility of converting the natives of other lands to their own religion. Columbus thus believed that it would be very easy to govern and mould such a gentle and mild-mannered tribe.

After spending a couple of days there, Columbus was intent to continue his journey to Cipango. Taking a few natives with him, the crew began their voyage again. The next few days, the crew went on discovering island after island. The islands now known as Long Island and Saometo were named *Fernandina* and *Isabella* respectively, by Columbus. Columbus' intention was however to reach Cipango. Through his communication with the natives, he understood that there were two larger islands, which they called Colba and Bofio. Columbus believed wrongly that Colba could be Cipango and Bofio was another larger island that was unknown to them.

The natives realized that these strangers were actually pursuing gold. Hence, they intimated that gold could be found on these larger islands. On October 28, the ships reached the island of Colba, or what is now known as Cuba. Columbus on arriving, renamed the island *Juana,* after the prince of Castile and Aragon, Don Juan. But he soon realized that it was not the island he was looking for, because its appearance did not fit the description of Cipango by Marco Polo.

Columbus sent his men to survey the island. They came back with reports of finding a large Indian village, made of several huts. But they couldn't find any gold anywhere on the island. This proved the natives wrong but Columbus did not let them go. This was due to the fact that on all the islands, the natives spoke the same language. Hence, he needed them for the purpose of communication. After coming to the conclusion that the island he was in was not Cipango, Columbus wrongly decided that he had reached the Asiatic mainland.

Columbus' purpose was to seek an audience with the Emperor of China, the Grand Khan. Mistakenly thinking that they had reached China, he inquired the natives about the Grand Khan. Due to their miscommunication, the natives interpreted this as a wish to meet their cacique, the chief of their tribe. Columbus sent his embassies along with the natives to the city where he believed the Grand Khan was present. Unfortunately, the men returned with the news of the reality that there was no Grand Khan but only a chief, named Guacanagari.

Disappointed by this news, Columbus decided to continue his journey to the next island, Bofio with the hope that

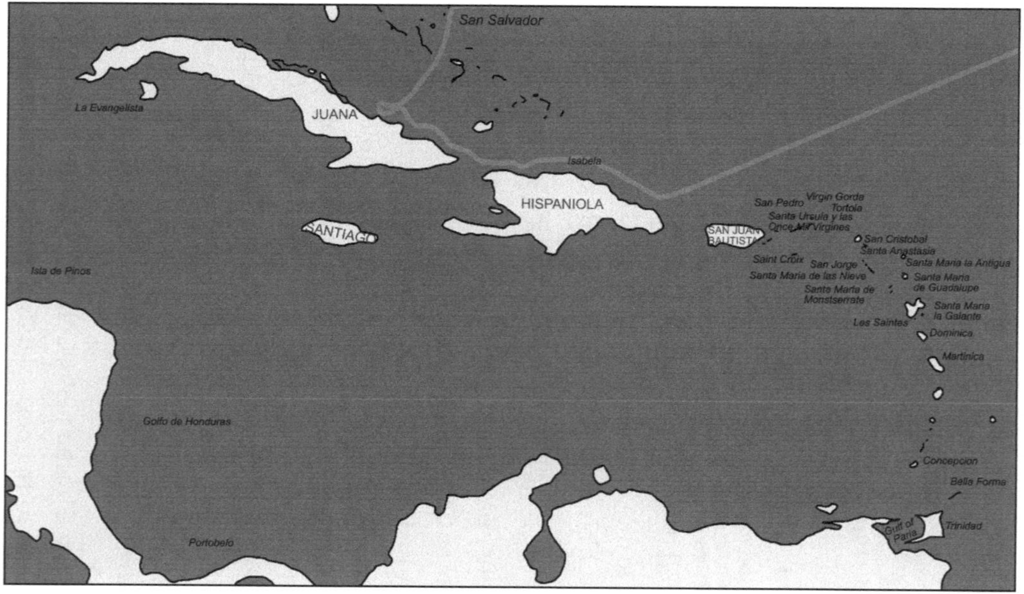

First Voyage

gold could be found there. This island now known as San Domingo or Haiti, was named *Hispaniola* by Columbus. Unfortunately, the *Santa Maria* hit a rock on the shore and was completely beyond repair. However, there was some good news as the Indians informed Columbus that there was indeed gold to be found on the island. This prompted him to build a settlement there. With the permission of the cacique, Columbus left some of his men in the settlement, which he named *La Navidad*. Disappointed at not having reached Cipango, he decided to return home.

On January 4, taking some Indians along with him, Columbus and the rest of the crew left on the remaining two ships. Columbus took command of the *Niña* . The return voyage was peaceful for most of the time but on February 13, a violent storm racked the sea. The dreadful weather tore the two ships asunder and the *Niña* lost sight of the *Pinta*. It was only on the February 18 that the ship could find land. Only Columbus could correctly conjecture that they had reached the Azores, a Portuguese archipelago.

The ship could continue its journey after February 22. However, by March 3, the ship again ran into rough weather. This time, it could lay anchor in the port of Lisbon. After what had passed between himself and the Portugal court, Columbus was not keen to land in Lisbon but he

Columbus before the Queen, imagined[33] by Emanuel Gottlieb Leutze, 1843

had no other alternative. Once the ship docked in Lisbon, Columbus sent an official communication to the King and the Queen of Spain regarding his discoveries. For nine days, the ship stayed there and started for Spain on March 13.

On March 15, the *Niña* landed in Palos. Amazingly, the *Pinta* which was supposed to have been lost in the storm, reached Palos the same evening. As news of the discoveries spread, Columbus was heralded with pomp and splendour. The monarchs replied graciously to his letter addressing him as 'Admiral of the Ocean Sea'. Columbus took the Indians and other birds, plants and trinkets from the new islands to Barcelona where the court was presently situated. The monarchs received him with honour. Most of his demands were met with. They even conferred the titles of *caballero* on his brothers, Bartholomew and Giacomo as per his wishes. Thus, it was no wonder that Columbus had no lack of support for his next voyage.

The Second Voyage

The success of Columbus' first voyage spurred the royal court of Spain to send the next expedition as early as possible. No stone was left unturned in equipping the voyage with the requisite ships, crew, provisions and ammunition. In a period of five months, seventeen vessels provided with stores, food, arms and ship gear for six months were prepared. The main purpose of the second voyage was to colonize the new lands with Spaniards.

Accordingly, everything that was needed to establish a colony of twelve to fifteen hundred men was loaded onto the ships. On 25 September 1493, the seventeen ships with nearly twelve hundred men aboard set sail from the port of

Cadiz. Unlike the first voyage, there was no hindrance in hiring men for the expedition. Columbus took his second brother, Giacomo along with him. On October 1, the fleet reached the Grand Canary. Here, the ships were loaded with livestock that would be needed in the new lands. Few days later, the fleet began its journey in a southwesterly course towards the discovered islands.

Before starting their voyage, Columbus gave each captain a sealed letter with instructions in case any ship lost touch with the others. However, that occasion did not arise throughout the whole journey.

On November 3, land was sighted. This time, the fleet had come upon the chain of islands in the Caribbean Sea. On the way to Hispaniola, the intended destination, Columbus discovered several islands. Among them are Dominica, Guadaloupe, Antigua, Saint Kitts, the Virgin Islands and Puerto Rico.

On November 22, the fleet finally reached the eastern coast of Hispaniola. Most of the crew which had not been on the first voyage was eager to see the settlement of La Navidad. One Indian who had been brought to Spain was sent ashore to present himself to the natives. He was dressed in new garb and had learnt Spanish very well. Unfortunately, after he left, there was no sign of him again.

Columbus then steered the fleet north towards the harbour of Monte Cristi. On arriving there on November 25, the voyagers' enthusiasm dampened considerably. On the shore, they found evidence of the death of the seamen who had stayed behind at the settlement. As more and more signs appeared of foul play, Columbus and his men realized that all had not been well at La Navidad.

Two days later, they reached the harbour of La Navidad. A cannon was fired as a sign of their arrival. But no corresponding reply was heard. The silence of the place intimated grim forebodings. However, the natives appeared as friendly as they were before. They informed the crew that most of the Spaniards had succumbed to disease while some had perished due to quarrels. Columbus did not find anything to cheer about when he saw the ruin and devastation of the settlement. Everything was broken and destroyed.

These signs prompted Columbus to establish a settlement elsewhere. They began to explore towards the east. However, it took them many days to counter the weather and find a suitable place. This delay also led to the livestock perishing and many men getting afflicted with disease. So, finally, on January 2, 1494, Columbus chose a spot and named it *Isabella* in the Queen's honour.

The establishment of the settlement was not an easy affair. The Spaniards had to struggle with stale provisions and the danger of disease and illness. They had to perform rigorous hard labour to build the houses there. The stressful work increased the discontent among the voyagers who had dreams of finding golden fortunes in Cipango and China. Columbus, burdened with these anxieties, fell prey to illness and was bedridden for several days.

The destruction of La Navidad distressed Columbus because this meant that no good reports about the settlement could be sent back to Spain. However, he did not sit back and idle. Instead, he sent two expeditions to search for any city or gold mine that he had heard so much about. The leaders of the expeditions were Ojeda and Gorvolan. Ojeda took the explorers across the mountainous region that surrounded Cibao. They found gold particles in the streams flowing from the mountains.

Deciding that it was enough evidence for the presence of gold, Ojeda returned with his expedition with the news. This was later corroborated by the second expedition. Columbus was heartened with this announcement. He decided to send back a glowing report to the monarchs. Twelve ships were fitted out to be sent to Spain. Along with letters to the Sovereigns, Columbus also requested that adequate provisions, implements and medications should be sent back immediately.

By the time the fleet left Hispaniola, Columbus had sufficiently recovered from illness. He decided to personally set forth for Cibao. On March 12, with most of his men on foot and horse, he started for Cibao. On the border of Cibao, he set up a fortress as a center for any mining operations that would be taken up. After establishing the plan for the fortress, which he named *Santo Tomas*, Columbus left it under the care of Pedro Margarit, an officer. With the rest of the men, he returned to Isabella by the end of March.

Soon after Columbus arrived at Isabella, a messenger from Santo Tomas informed that the fort was going to be attacked by a cacique of another tribe, Caonabo. Columbus sent some of his men to help Margarit defend the fort. Before venturing into further exploration, he sought to put the settlement into order. However, the men, tired and stressed under the work routine, were almost on the verge of rebellion. Columbus decided that it was important to continue his exploration in order to quell the growing discontent.

On April 24, leaving Giacomo in charge of Isabella, Columbus and his men set out for Cuba and other lands.

The other reason for this venture was the fact that John II was sending voyagers to reach India through east. So it was a matter of prestige between the two nations, Portugal and Spain on who would establish trade route to the Indies by sea. When Columbus and his crew began to sail along the coast, he started believing that Cuba was not an island but a peninsula. Like his earlier assumptions, he thought that Cuba was a part of the Asian mainland.

As the expedition continued, they reached the island of Jamaica on May 5. Columbus named the harbour they landed on, St Ann's Bay, as *Santa Gloria*. He also discovered a group of islands along the south shore of Cuba. He named them *the Queen's Garden*. As the journey resumed, several times the ships ran aground or were stuck in mud. Fortunately, they did not suffer too much damage.

Meanwhile, Columbus began to formulate an extravagant plan. He thought that he would be able to travel further and reach the Indian Ocean. He believed he would be able to reach Spain by rounding the Cape of Good Hope.

Though the plan was highly imaginative, Columbus knew the practical difficulties of implementing it. First, the ships were not in a condition to chart such a perilous journey. Secondly, the crew were tired, distressed and scared that they would never be able to return to Hispaniola. By June

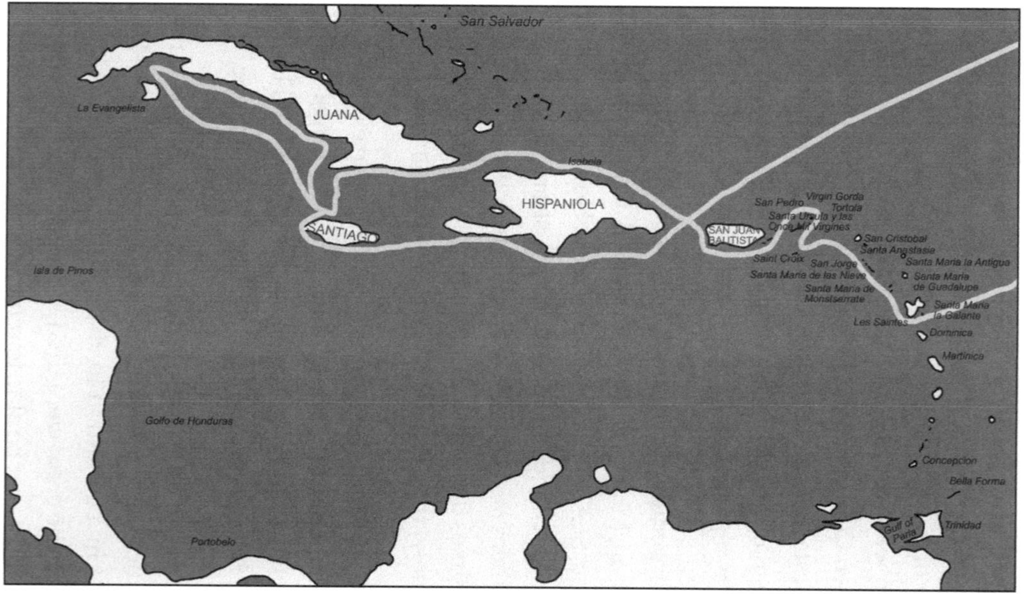

Second Voyage

12, the crew had had enough of exploration. Columbus could not risk going any further with a discontented crew. So he decided to turn back. But it was a matter of shame and regret for him for having failed to reach the mainland of China.

In order to avoid getting the blame for not going any further, Columbus made his men swear to a written statement saying Cuba was a peninsula and it would be possible to reach Spain from there by land and sea. The expedition then turned its course back to Isabella. It finally reached the settlement on September 29. During the return journey, Columbus once again fell ill. Even after they reached Isabella, his illness did not subside. But luckily for him, his brother, Bartholomew had arrived at Isabella sometime before. He was sent by the Sovereigns with three caravels loaded with the supplies that Columbus had requested for.

Columbus who had nothing much to cheer about from his expedition, found that matters were not any pleasant at Isabella either. The settlement which he had left in the hands of his brother, Giacomo, was in a state of absolute anarchy. The hitherto friendly relations between the natives and the foreigners were now strained. A great part of this was due to the excesses and greed of the Spaniards. Unable to bear the atrocious behaviour of the foreigners, the natives under the leadership of two caciques began an assault on Isabella and Santo Tomas.

The natives, however were no match to the armed Spaniards. Most of them were killed while the caciques were also taken captive. Thus the foreigners had absolute control over the land. The natives were now completely subjugated. Four more forts were built in order to gain command over the whole land. Apart from this, Columbus passed an order that forced the natives to pay either a bellful of gold or twenty-five pounds of cotton every three months.

These conditions were almost impossible to fulfill. The natives faced several consequent discriminations which led to their tribe being subjected to terror, famine and disease. Most of the natives were wiped out and the remaining were forced to be servile to the foreigners. Meanwhile, Columbus was not faring any better with his own men. The voyagers became increasingly bitter as they were pushed to work hard with hardly any sustenance. Moreover, the authority that Columbus gave to his two brothers also led to discontent and distrust among the men.

As conditions worsened, the news of the chaos at Isabella reached the ears of the Sovereigns through the officer, Margarit. Margarit who was in charge of Santo Tomas had long before abandoned the fortress and had reached Spain. Thus, the monarchs had to institute a commission to know the real state of affairs in the islands. Don John Agnado was sent as the commissioner with four caravels to the settlement in Hispaniola.

When the commissioner arrived, the embittered Spaniards poured their woes to him. Columbus knew that his position would be in grave danger if the commissioner sent his report based on the events occurring there. He decided that he had to go back to Spain immediately in order to present his own case in front of the monarchs. However, a severe hurricane had destroyed the four caravels brought by Agnado. Also, reports of existence of gold mines in the southern coast were received.

Columbus built a fort, by the name of *San Cristobal,* near the supposed location of the mine. Only after that was he able to depart with some of his men to Spain. Columbus and Agnado took charge of the remaining two ships and set sail for Spain on March 10, 1496. The men who came on board these ships were the ghosts of their previous selves. The enthusiasm and curiosity had completely died and the men were exhausted, distraught and weakened by illness and hunger. After a travel of three months, the two ships finally reached Cadiz on June 11.

The Third Voyage

The arrival of the two ships was met with a reception that was contrary to the great farewell the expedition had been given on its departure. Most of the men who had embarked on the journey had either succumbed to disease or hunger. Even the promise of discovery of fortunes of gold was not fulfilled.

When Columbus reached Cadiz, three ships were setting sail with provisions for the island. Through them, he sent a message to his brother, intimating his safe arrival and also urging him to ensure that progress was made in the stability of the colony's affairs and the discovery of gold mines.

Columbus received an invitation from the Sovereigns to meet them at Almazan. He arrived there with whatever gold and treasures he had gathered in the islands. Though there were vicious reports against him, the monarchs received Columbus kindly. They assured him that some of his demands which had not been fulfilled after the first voyage would be taken care of. Among such assurances, Columbus did not have much to fear about.

However, the conditions in Spain were soon going to divert the attention of the monarchs from the maritime expeditions. During the next two years, the country was at war with France. Also, matrimonial alliances for the royal children with England and Austria were under way. Hence, most of the royal ships were engaged in these affairs. Columbus had to wait for a long time before he could press the need for the third voyage.

When Columbus applied to the Queen, she agreed to send two caravels loaded with supplies in February 1498. But Columbus had to face more delays before he could embark on the third voyage. It was only on May 30 that he could begin his journey with six ships. After reaching the Canary Islands on July 5, he decided to send three of the ships to Hispaniola with the supplies and to take the other three ships to explore the southwest.

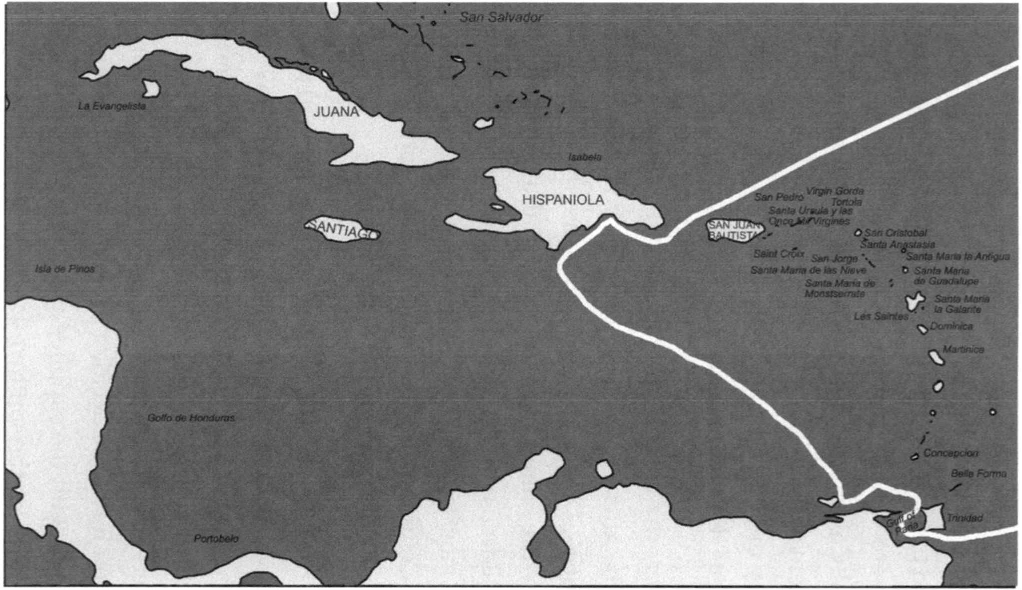

Third Voyage

As the three ships travelled in the southwesterly direction, they had to face severe temperatures which forced Columbus to abandon the exploration and head back to Hispaniola. As they began sailing to the northwest, he discovered the islands of Trinidad and Tobago and explored the Gulf of Paria. The ships came to Hispaniola by the end of August.

During the period that Columbus was away from Isabella, Bartholomew was left in charge of the settlement. His first duty was to take care of the fort, San Cristobal where workmen often discovered pieces of gold while digging. The ships which had arrived with provisions were sent back with the natives who had been captured at several times during their stay. The transfer of natives to Spain had slowly developed into a slave trade.

Bartholomew began to shift his men from Isabella to the site where the gold mines were supposed to be located, the river Ozama. Here, he built a fort named *Santo Domingo*. It was then that he was taken up with the idea of exploring a western Indian kingdom, Xaragua. This was an unnecessary diversion. While he was away in Xaragua, a mutiny was slowly building against him in Isabella.

The men were disappointed by the lack of new discovery of gold, the shortage of supplies from Spain and the leadership of a foreigner, Bartholomew. The disgruntled men were headed by Francis Roldan, who had been appointed earlier by Columbus as the chief justice of the island. When Bartholomew returned to Isabella, he faced the prospect of rebellion. But at that juncture, the three ships sent from Canary Islands arrived. The ships brought the royal confirmation of Bartholomew's authority. Roldan and seventy rebels escaped to Xaragua. It was in these conditions that Columbus returned to Hispaniola.

After Columbus' return, he tried to come to an agreement with Roldan and the rebels. According to the treaty, Columbus agreed to several conditions put forward by Roldan. For some time, there was momentary peace on the island. But the harmony did not last long. Columbus faced stiff opposition from another instigator, Ojeda. The news of the tumultuous atmosphere soon reached Spain.

The reputation of Columbus received a severe beating. The process of sending the natives as slaves was not much appreciated by the Queen. Apart from this, there were reports of the revolt and the disappointment of not finding as much gold as was predicted.

The monarchs were soon reconsidering their opinion on Columbus. On March 21, 1499, they instituted a commission under Francis de Bobadilla, investing in him many powers, including authority over Columbus. However, it was not until July 1500 that Bobadilla arrived at Isabella. Sadly, by the time he was there, conditions had so worsened that Columbus had ordered the execution of some of the rebels.

When Bobadilla landed at Isabella, Columbus and Bartholomew were at another part of the island. Giacomo was in charge of Isabella. Bobadilla asserted his authority and stopped the further executions. The men at Isabella saw an opportunity to air their grievances and Bobadilla, justly or unjustly took away all powers and property from the hands of Columbus. When Columbus returned, he and his brothers were put in jail.

By October, Columbus and his brothers, chained and manacled were sent in a ship back to Spain. Whether his conduct with the natives or poor governance warranted this kind of punishment cannot be proven but he was definitely not a success as an administrator. Thus, he arrived back at Cadiz on November 1500 in this state of disgrace.

The Final Voyage

Irrespective of what had led to his arrest, the appearance of Columbus in chains had an immediate effect on the people of Spain. The popular opinion veered towards sympathy and pity for the great Admiral who was brought in disgrace due to the overweening authority of Bobadilla. The monarchs who had given these powers to Bobadilla however did not endorse his actions. On hearing the gross injustice done to a respected figure like Columbus, the Sovereigns instantly secured his release and invited him to court with due honour.

In the presence of the monarchs, Columbus put forward his explanations, stressing on the various hardships he had undergone during the voyages. He regarded his failures in governance due to lack of experience and the extreme strain of problems he encountered. The Queen in her speech declared that she never lost faith in Columbus as an Admiral. But the unsavoury reports against him had compelled her to appoint a commission. She was especially dissatisfied with the way Columbus had treated the natives. However, she understood that Bobadilla had acted without discretion.

Columbus now wanted to be reinstated as the governor and head of all the islands. But here, the King was reluctant to consider his request. The settlement had not prospered in any way desirable by the monarchs. The quantity of gold brought to Spain did not match the expectations. Moreover, in the past few years, several notable explorers had made more advances and lucrative expeditions than Columbus. Hence, the King was not in a hurry to give monopoly over the many islands to a single man. The decision finally taken was to entrust Columbus with a new expedition and appoint a new governor for the islands.

The new governor, Nicholas de Ovando, was sent to Hispaniola with the largest fleet till then - thirty ships with nearly twenty-five hundred on board. Columbus now was intent to find a way through the west to the Indian Ocean.

With four ships and Bartholomew and his son, Fernando in tow, Columbus set sail from Cadiz on May 9, 1502. On the way, the ships were in the midst of an impending hurricane. Hence, Columbus landed at Santo Domingo and requested Ovando to give his fleet temporary shelter.

For reasons unknown, Ovando refused to comply with Columbus' request. Apart from that, he did not agree with Columbus' prediction of the hurricane. As a result, a great number of ships carrying a substantial amount of gold and men like Bobadilla and Roldan left for Spain. Columbus managed to find a small shelter for his ships in the island. But as he had predicted, a tremendous hurricane struck the ships on June 30.

The storm battered the ships for several days but eventually, none of the ships was lost. The same could not be said about the fleet bound for Spain. Only four ships survived and all the important men on board perished at sea. Three of the ships returned to Santo Domingo and only one ship, which was carrying Columbus' share of the gold reached Spain.

After the storm had subsided, Columbus resumed sailing in a southwesterly direction and reached Honduras in August. As they continued their journey south, the ships faced severe storms for nearly twenty-eight days. The ships

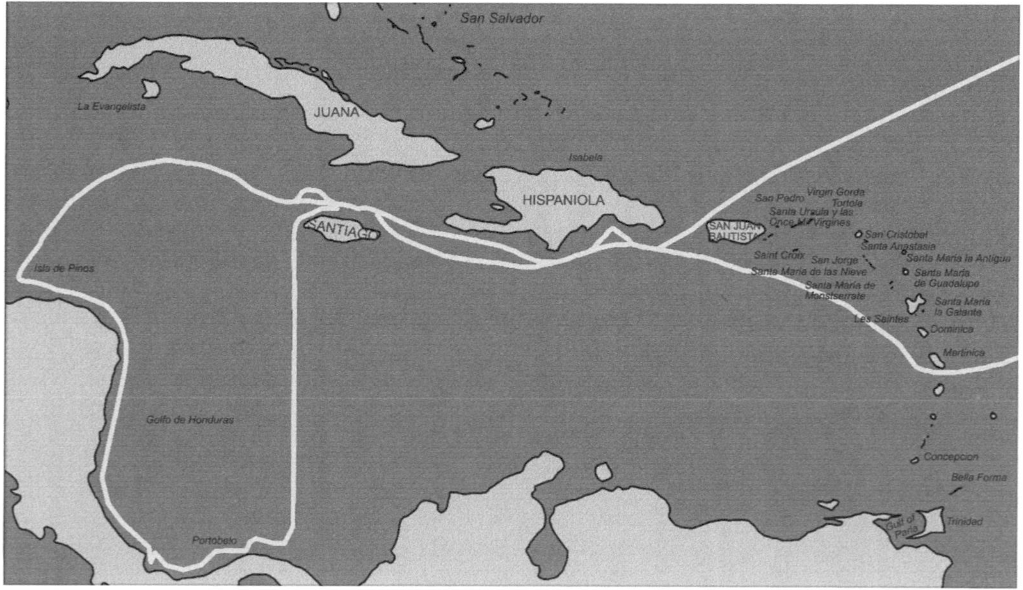

Fourth and the final Voyage

stayed close to the shore throughout their course. The storm finally subsided on September 14 when the ships rounded a cape, named by Columbus as *Cape Gracias á Dios*. The next few days, the fleet passed through Nicaragua and Costa Rica.

As the voyage continued south, no significant developments occurred. The ships were battered by the tiresome journey and the provisions had become mouldy. So Columbus was forced to go back the way they had come. As they turned back, the ships once again were caught in an unforeseen tempest. The whole winter passed by as the fleet battled severe storms. Only on January 7, 1503, the ships could find anchor near the river Rio Belen.

Columbus decided to stay put there until the weather improved. Fortunately, the exploration of this place was more fruitful. Columbus discovered that gold was found here more in abundance than in Hispaniola. So a settlement was established there but it did not fare any better. By April, the Spaniards were under the strain of an attack by the natives and also inclement weather. With just two caravels left, Columbus and his men were forced to turn back to Hispaniola.

On the way to Hispaniola, the ships once again were battered by a storm near the coast of Cuba. The fleet finally

Columbus intimidates natives by predicting lunar eclipse

found shelter in Jamaica on June 25. But the conditions did not improve for the crew. The natives were not friendly and the supplies were diminishing. Columbus decided to send one of his men, Diego Mendez to Ovando seeking help. While Mendez and some men were on their way, Columbus was struck by illness. The months passed by and the relations with the natives deteriorated.

By February 1504, Columbus and his men were facing a host of problems. It was then that Columbus used his knowledge to influence the natives. Being aware that a lunar eclipse was in the offing, he sent out a message to the natives that the heavens were displeased with them. Only when the natives satisfied the Spaniards would the Gods be happy. When the moon disappeared, the natives were convinced with Columbus' assertions. From then on, there was no shortage of supplies for the men. However, help from Ovando did not arrive until June 25, 1504, a year after they had reached Jamaica.

Eventually, Columbus and his men reached Santo Domingo on August 15. But differences between Columbus and Ovando meant that the former had to leave for Spain by the next month. With two ships and his brother and son, Columbus reached the port of San Lucar in Spain by November 7.

Columbus' tomb in Seville Cathedral.

The Journey Ends

The fourth voyage undertaken by Columbus would be his last adventure on sea. By the time he returned to Spain, his health had succumbed to the rigorous sea life he had lived for several years. He travelled with the court of the monarchs from Seville to Salamanca and finally to Valladodid. On May 20, 1506, he breathed his last.

The last year and half that Columbus was at home was spent in leisure. Having become a wealthy man, due to his share of gold from Hispaniola, he gave up his time in recording his experiences, efforts and difficulties. Till the day he died, he never doubted that the islands he had found were not a part of Asia, as he fervently believed.

Though Columbus' death did not create a stir during his time, his life and adventures left behind a great legacy. To date, this fifteenth-century seaman is celebrated and feted as a pioneer. October 12, the day he first landed on the American continent, is commemorated in many states of America as *Columbus Day*. Several cities, towns and even capitals of US states have been named in his honour.

Like many other personalities, the character of Columbus has received both praise and censure. While his adventurous spirit is applauded, his attitude towards the Native Americans which resulted in their near annihilation is often debated upon.

The reasons that drove the man towards exploration - whether it was a search for gold, a quest for religious conversions, the desire to earn name and fame for himself - are secondary. The predominant factor that should be remembered was his passion and courage to push the boundaries and discover the unknown.

In his life, Columbus achieved what was supposed improbable. He persevered even when he was derided, denounced and defeated by his critics. He may not have been a perfect administrator but his voyages towards the unknown are a testimony to his determination, fervour and bravery.

Hi story gives inspiration to the one who wonders what lies beyond the horizon and hopes to conquer the seas in search of the unknown. Columbus might have lived many centuries ago but his life remains a beacon of hope to anyone who dares to think beyond the possible.

Prodigy books

Biographies

Abdul Kalam
Charles Darwin
Marie Curie
Visvesvaraya
Srinivasa Ramanujan
Newton
Einstein
James Watt
Sir JC Bose
Alexander Graham Bell
Gandhi
Jawaharlal Nehru
Mother Teresa
Ambedkar
Bhagat Sigh
Tipu Sultan
Rani of Jhansi
Akbar
Shivaji
Bharati
Rabindranath Tagore
Martin Luther King
Alexander the Great
Napoleon
Adolf Hitler
Charlie Chaplin
Walt Disney
Bill Gates
Narayana Murthy
Columbus

Classics Retold

Homer's Iliad
The Odyssey
The Tempest
Hamlet
The Merchant of Venice
Twelfth Night
Romeo and Juliet
Macbeth

Other Titles

The Universe
Hinduism
Global Warming
Abraham Lincoln
The New 7 wonders of the World
Life
Tsunami
Dinosaurs
Ganga
World War II
Madras - Chennai
Exam Tips
Television
Effective Communication
Creative Thinking